Old Times

Harold Pinter was born in London in 1930. He is married to Antonia Fraser. In 1995 he won the David Cohen British Literature Prize, awarded for a lifetime's achievement in literature. In 1996 he was given the Laurence Olivier Award for a lifetime's achievement in theatre. In 2002 he was made a Companion of Honour for services to literature.

HAROLD PINTER

Old Times

ff

faber and faber

First published by Eyre Methuen Limited in 1971.
Reprinted by Faber and Faber Limited in 1988.
This edition first published in 2004
by Faber and Faber Limited
3 Queen Square, London WC1N 3AU

Typeset by Country Setting, Kingsdown, Kent CT14 8ES
Printed in England by Mackays of Chatham plc, Chatham, Kent

The right of Harold Pinter to be identified as author
of this work has been asserted in accordance with Section 77
of the Copyright, Designs and Patents Act 1988

A CIP record for this book
is available from the British Library

ISBN 0-571-22563-2

2 4 6 8 10 9 7 5 3 1

To Peter Hall

Old Times was first presented by the Royal
Shakespeare Company at the Aldwych Theatre,
London, on 1 June 1971, with the following cast:

DEELEY   Colin Blakely
KATE   Dorothy Tutin
ANNA   Vivien Merchant

Directed by Peter Hall

The play was produced for television by the BBC in
October 1975, with the following cast:

DEELEY   Barry Foster
KATE   Anna Cropper
ANNA   Mary Miller

Directed by Christopher Morahan

It was produced at the Theatre Royal, Haymarket,
London, in April 1985 with the following cast:

DEELEY   Michael Gambon
KATE   Nicola Pagett
ANNA   Liv Ullman

Directed by David Jones

The play was revived for television by the BBC in 1991, with the following cast:

DEELEY	John Malkovich
KATE	Kate Nelligan
ANNA	Miranda Richardson

Directed by Simon Curtis

It was revived at Wyndham's Theatre, London, in July 1995, with the following cast:

DEELEY	Leigh Lawson
KATE	Julie Christie
ANNA	Harriet Walter

Directed by Lindy Davies

It was revived at the Donmar Warehouse, London, in July 2004, with the following cast:

DEELEY	Jeremy Northam
KATE	Gina McKee
ANNA	Helen McCrory

Directed by Roger Michell

Characters

Deeley

Kate

Anna

All in their early forties

OLD TIMES

A converted farmhouse.

A long window up centre. Bedroom door up left.
Front door up right.

Spare modern furniture.
Two sofas. An armchair.

Autumn. Night.

Act One

Light dim. Three figures discovered.

DEELEY *slumped in armchair, still.*
KATE *curled on a sofa, still.*
ANNA *standing at the window, looking out.*

Silence.

Lights up on DEELEY *and* KATE, *smoking cigarettes.*

ANNA's *figure remains still in dim light at the window.*

> KATE
> (*reflectively*)

Dark

Pause.

> DEELEY

Fat or thin?

> KATE

Fuller than me. I think.

Pause.

> DEELEY

She was then?

KATE

I think so.

DEELEY

She may not be now.

Pause.

Was she your best friend?

KATE

Oh, what does that mean?

DEELEY

What?

KATE

The word friend . . . when you look back . . . all that time.

DEELEY

Can't you remember what you felt?

Pause.

KATE

It is a very long time.

DEELEY

But you remember her. She remembers you. Or why would she be coming here tonight?

KATE

I suppose because she remembers me.

Pause.

DEELEY

Did you *think* of her as your best friend?

KATE

She was my only friend.

DEELEY

Your best and only.

KATE

My one and only.

Pause.

If you have only one of something you can't say it's
the best of anything.

DEELEY

Because you have nothing to compare it with?

KATE

Mmnn.

Pause.

DEELEY
(*smiling*)

She was incomparable.

KATE

Oh, I'm sure she wasn't.

Pause.

DEELEY

I didn't know you had so few friends.

KATE

I had none. None at all. Except her.

DEELEY

Why her?

KATE

I don't know.

Pause.

She was a thief. She used to steal things.

DEELEY

Who from?

KATE

Me.

DEELEY

What things?

KATE

Bits and pieces. Underwear.

DEELEY *chuckles.*

DEELEY

Will you remind her?

KATE

Oh . . . I don't think so.

Pause.

DEELEY

Is that what attracted you to her?

KATE

What?

DEELEY

The fact that she was a thief.

6

KATE

No.

Pause.

DEELEY

Are you looking forward to seeing her?

KATE

No.

DEELEY

I am. I shall be very interested.

KATE

In what?

DEELEY

In you. I'll be watching you.

KATE

Me? Why?

DEELEY

To see if she's the same person.

KATE

You think you'll find that out through me?

DEELEY

Definitely.

Pause.

KATE

I hardly remember her. I've almost totally forgotten
her.

Pause.

DEELEY

Any idea what she drinks?

KATE

None.

DEELEY

She may be a vegetarian.

KATE

Ask her.

DEELEY

It's too late. You've cooked your casserole.

Pause.

Why isn't she married? I mean, why isn't she bringing her husband?

KATE

Ask her.

DEELEY

Do I have to ask her everything?

KATE

Do you want me to ask your questions for you?

DEELEY

No. Not at all.

Pause.

KATE

Of course she's married.

DEELEY

How do you know?

8

KATE

Everyone's married.

DEELEY

Then why isn't she bringing her husband?

KATE

Isn't she?

Pause.

DEELEY

Did she mention a husband in her letter?

KATE

No.

DEELEY

What do you think he'd be like? I mean, what sort of man would she have married? After all, she was your best – your only – friend. You must have some idea. What kind of man would he be?

KATE

I have no idea.

DEELEY

Haven't you any curiosity?

KATE

You forget. I know her.

DEELEY

You haven't seen her for twenty years.

KATE

You've never seen her. There's a difference.

Pause.

DEELEY
At least the casserole is big enough for four.

KATE
You said she was a vegetarian.

Pause.

DEELEY
Did *she* have many friends?

KATE
Oh . . . the normal amount, I suppose.

DEELEY
Normal? What's normal? You had none.

KATE
One.

DEELEY
Is that normal?

Pause.

She . . . had quite a lot of friends, did she?

KATE
Hundreds.

DEELEY
You met them?

KATE
Not all, I think. But after all, we were living together.
There were visitors, from time to time. I met them.

DEELEY

Her visitors?

KATE

What?

DEELEY

Her visitors. Her friends. You had no friends.

KATE

Her friends, yes.

DEELEY

You met them.

Pause.

(*abruptly*) You lived together?

KATE

Mmmnn?

DEELEY

You lived together?

KATE

Of course.

DEELEY

I didn't know that.

KATE

Didn't you?

DEELEY

You never told me that. I thought you just knew each other.

KATE

We did.

DEELEY

But in fact you lived with each other.

KATE

Of course we did. How else would she steal my
underwear from me? In the street?

Pause.

DEELEY

I knew you had shared with someone at one time . . .

Pause.

But I didn't know it was her.

KATE

Of course it was.

Pause.

DEELEY

Anyway, none of this matters.

ANNA *turns from the window, speaking, and moves
down to them, eventually sitting on the second sofa.*

ANNA

Queuing all night, the rain, do you remember? my
goodness, the Albert Hall, Covent Garden, what did
we eat? to look back, half the night, to do things we
loved, we were young then of course, but what stamina,
and to work in the morning, and to a concert, or the
opera, or the ballet, that night, you haven't forgotten?
and then riding on top of the bus down Kensington

High Street, and the bus conductors, and then dashing for the matches for the gas fire and then I suppose scrambled eggs, or did we? who cooked? both giggling and chattering, both huddling to the heat, then bed and sleeping, and all the hustle and bustle in the morning, rushing for the bus again for work, lunchtimes in Green Park, exchanging all our news, with our very own sandwiches, innocent girls, innocent secretaries, and then the night to come, and goodness knows what excitement in store, I mean the sheer expectation of it all, the looking-forwardness of it all, and so poor, but to be poor and young, and a girl, in London then . . . and the cafés we found, almost private ones, weren't they? where artists and writers and sometimes actors collected, and others with dancers, we sat hardly breathing with our coffee, heads bent, so as not to be seen, so as not to disturb, so as not to distract, and listened and listened to all those words, all those cafés and all those people, creative undoubtedly, and does it still exist I wonder? do you know? can you tell me?

Slight pause.

DEELEY

We rarely get to London.

KATE *stands, goes to a small table and pours coffee from a pot.*

KATE

Yes, I remember.

She adds milk and sugar to one cup and takes it to ANNA. *She takes a black coffee to* DEELEY *and then sits with her own.*

DEELEY
(*to* ANNA)

Do you drink brandy?

ANNA

I would love some brandy.

DEELEY *pours brandy for all and hands the glasses.*
He remains standing with his own.

ANNA

Listen. What silence. Is it always as silent?

DEELEY

It's quite silent here, yes. Normally.

Pause.

You can hear the sea sometimes if you listen very
carefully.

ANNA

How wise you were to choose this part of the world,
and how sensible and courageous of you both to stay
permanently in such a silence.

DEELEY

My work takes me away quite often, of course. But
Kate stays here.

ANNA

No one who lived here would want to go far. I would
not want to go far, I would be afraid of going far, lest
when I returned the house would be gone.

DEELEY

Lest?

ANNA

What?

DEELEY

The word lest. Haven't heard it for a long time.

Pause.

KATE

Sometimes I walk to the sea. There aren't many
people. It's a long beach.

Pause.

ANNA

But I would miss London, nevertheless. But of course
I was a girl in London. We were girls together.

DEELEY

I wish I had known you both then.

ANNA

Do you?

DEELEY

Yes.

DEELEY *pours more brandy for himself.*

ANNA

You have a wonderful casserole.

DEELEY

What?

ANNA

I mean wife. So sorry. A wonderful wife.

Ah.

I was referring to the casserole. I was referring to your wife's cooking,

You're not a vegetarian, then?

No. Oh no.

Yes, you need good food in the country, substantial food, to keep you going, all the air . . . you know.

Pause.

Yes, I quite like those kind of things, doing it.

What kind of things?

Oh, you know, that sort of thing.

Pause.

Do you mean cooking?

All that thing.

We weren't terribly elaborate in cooking, didn't have the time, but every so often dished up an incredibly enormous stew, guzzled the lot, and then more often than not sat up half the night reading Yeats.

Pause.

(*to herself*) Yes. Every so often. More often than not.

ANNA *stands, walks to the window.*

And the sky is so still.

Pause.

Can you see that tiny ribbon of light? Is that the sea? Is that the horizon?

DEELEY
You live on a very different coast.

ANNA
Oh, very different. I live on a volcanic island.

DEELEY
I know it.

ANNA
Oh, do you?

DEELEY
I've been there.

Pause.

ANNA
I'm so delighted to be here.

DEELEY
It's nice I know for Katey to see you. She hasn't many friends.

ANNA

She has you.

DEELEY

She hasn't made many friends, although there's been every opportunity for her to do so.

ANNA

Perhaps she has all she wants.

DEELEY

She lacks curiosity.

ANNA

Perhaps she's happy.

Pause.

KATE

Are you talking about me?

DEELEY

Yes.

ANNA

She was always a dreamer.

DEELEY

She likes taking long walks. All that. You know. Raincoat on. Off down the lane, hands deep in pockets. All that kind of thing.

ANNA *turns to look at* KATE.

ANNA

Yes.

DEELEY

Sometimes I take her face in my hands and look at it.

ANNA

Really?

DEELEY

Yes, I look at it, holding it in my hands. Then I kind
of let it go, take my hands away, leave it floating.

KATE

My head is quite fixed. I have it on.

DEELEY
(*to* ANNA)

It just floats away.

ANNA

She was always a dreamer.

ANNA *sits*.

Sometimes, walking, in the park, I'd say to her, you're
dreaming, you're dreaming, wake up, what are you
dreaming? and she'd look round at me, flicking her
hair, and look at me as if I were part of her dream.

Pause.

One day she said to me, I've slept through Friday. No
you haven't, I said, what do you mean? I've slept right
through Friday, she said. But today is Friday, I said,
it's been Friday all day, it's now Friday night, you
haven't slept through Friday. Yes I have, she said, I've
slept right through it, today is Saturday.

DEELEY

You mean she literally didn't know what day it was?

ANNA

No.

KATE

Yes I did. It was Saturday.

Pause.

DEELEY

What month are we in?

KATE

September.

Pause.

DEELEY

We're forcing her to think. We must see you more
often. You're a healthy influence.

ANNA

But she was always a charming companion.

DEELEY

Fun to live with?

ANNA

Delightful.

DEELEY

Lovely to look at, delightful to know.

ANNA

Ah, those songs. We used to play them, all of them,
all the time, he at night, lying on the floor, lovely old
things. Sometimes I'd look at her face, but she was
quite unaware of my gaze.

DEELEY

Gaze?

ANNA

What?

DEELEY

The word gaze. Don't hear it very often.

ANNA

Yes, quite unaware of it. She was totally absorbed.

DEELEY

In 'Lovely to look at, delightful to know?'

KATE
(*to* ANNA)
I don't know that song. Did we have it?

DEELEY
(*singing, to* KATE)
You're lovely to look at, delightful to know . . .

ANNA

Oh we did. Yes, of course. We had them all.

DEELEY
(*singing*)
Blue moon, I see you standing alone . . .

ANNA
(*singing*)
The way you comb your hair . . .

DEELEY
(*singing*)
Oh no they can't take that away from me . . .

ANNA
(*singing*)
Oh but you're lovely, with your smile so warm . . .

DEELEY
(*singing*)
I've got a woman crazy for me.
She's funny that way.

Slight pause.

ANNA
(*singing*)
You are the promised kiss of springtime . . .

DEELEY
(*singing*)
And someday I'll know that moment divine,
When all the things you are, are mine!

Slight pause.

ANNA
(*singing*)
I get no kick from champagne,
Mere alcohol doesn't thrill me at all,
So tell me why should it be true –

DEELEY
(*singing*)
That I get a kick out of you?

Pause.

ANNA
(*singing*)
They asked me how I knew
My true love was true,

I of course replied,
Something here inside
Cannot be denied.

DEELEY
(*singing*)
When a lovely flame dies . . .

ANNA
(*singing*)
Smoke gets in your eyes.

Pause.

DEELEY
(*singing*)
The sigh of midnight trains in empty stations . . .

Pause.

ANNA
(*singing*)
The park at evening when the bell has sounded . . .

Pause.

DEELEY
(*singing*)
The smile of Garbo and the scent of roses . . .

ANNA
(*singing*)
The waiters whistling as the last bar closes . . .

DEELEY
(*singing*)
Oh, how the ghost of you clings . . .

Pause.

They don't make them like that any more.

Silence.

What happened to me was this. I popped into a fleapit to see *Odd Man Out*. Some bloody awful summer afternoon, walking in no direction. I remember thinking there was something familiar about the neighbourhood and suddenly recalled that it was in this very neighbourhood that my father bought me my first tricycle, the only tricycle in fact I ever possessed. Anyway, there was the bicycle shop and there was this fleapit showing *Odd Man Out* and there were two usherettes standing in the foyer and one of them was stroking her breasts and the other one was saying 'dirty bitch' and the one stroking her breasts was saying 'mmnnn' with a very sensual relish and smiling at her fellow usherette, so I marched in on this excruciatingly hot summer afternoon in the middle of nowhere and watched *Odd Man Out* and thought Robert Newton was fantastic. And I still think he was fantastic. And I would commit murder for him, even now. And there was only one other person in the cinema, one other person in the whole of the whole cinema, and there she is. And there she was, very dim, very still, placed more or less I would say at the dead centre of the auditorium. I was off centre and have remained so. And I left when the film was over, noticing, even though James Mason was dead, that the first usherette appeared to be utterly exhausted, and I stood for a moment in the sun, thinking I suppose about something and then this girl came out

and I think looked about her and I said wasn't Robert
Newton fantastic, and she said something or other,
Christ knows what, but looked at me, and I thought
Jesus this is it, I've made a catch, this is a true-blue
pickup, and when we had sat down in the café with
tea she looked into her cup and then up at me and
told me she thought Robert Newton was remarkable.
So it was Robert Newton who brought us together
and it is only Robert Newton who can tear us apart.

Pause.

ANNA

F. J. McCormick was good too.

DEELEY

I know F. J. McCormick was good too. But he didn't
bring us together.

Pause.

You've seen the film then?

ANNA

Yes.

DEELEY

When?

ANNA

Oh . . . long ago.

Pause.

DEELEY
(*to* KATE)

Remember that film?

KATE

Oh yes. Very well.

Pause.

DEELEY

I think I am right in saying the next time we met we
held hands. I held her cool hand, as she walked by
me, and I said something which made her smile, and
she looked at me, didn't you, flicking her hair back,
and I thought she was even more fantastic than
Robert Newton.

Pause.

And then at a slightly later stage our naked bodies met,
hers cool, warm, highly agreeable, and I wondered
what Robert Newton would think of this. What would
he think of this I wondered as I touched her profoundly
all over. (*to* ANNA) What do you think he'd think?

ANNA

I never met Robert Newton but I do know I know
what you mean. There are some things one remembers
even though they may never have happened. There
are things I remember which may never have
happened but as I recall them so they take place.

DEELEY

What?

ANNA

This man crying in our room. One night late I returned
and found him sobbing, his hand over his face, sitting
in the armchair, all crumpled in the armchair and
Katey sitting on the bed with a mug of coffee and

no one spoke to me, no one spoke, no one looked up. There was nothing I could do. I undressed and switched out the light and got into my bed, the curtains were thin, the light from the street came in, Katey still, on her bed, the man sobbed, the light came in, it flicked the wall, there was a slight breeze, the curtains occasionally shook, there was nothing but sobbing, suddenly it stopped. The man came over to me, quickly, looked down at me, but I would have absolutely nothing to do with him, nothing.

Pause.

No, no, I'm quite wrong . . . he didn't move quickly . . . that's quite wrong . . . he moved . . . very slowly, the light was bad, and stopped. He stood in the centre of the room. He looked at us both, at our beds. Then he turned towards me. He approached my bed. He bent down over me. But I would have nothing to do with him, absolutely nothing.

Pause.

DEELEY
What kind of man was he?

ANNA
But after a while I heard him go out. I heard the front door close, and footsteps in the street, then silence, then the footsteps fade away, and then silence.

Pause.

But then sometime later in the night I woke up and looked across the room to her bed and saw two shapes.

DEELEY

He'd come back!

ANNA

He was lying across her lap on her bed.

DEELEY

A man in the dark across my wife's lap?

Pause.

ANNA

But then in the early morning . . . he had gone.

DEELEY

Thank Christ for that.

ANNA

It was as if he had never been.

DEELEY

Of course he'd been. He went twice and came once.

Pause.

Well, what an exciting story that was.

Pause.

What did he look like, this fellow?

ANNA

Oh, I never saw his face clearly. I don't know.

DEELEY

But was he –?

KATE *stands. She goes to a small table, takes a cigarette from a box and lights it. She looks down at* ANNA.

KATE

You talk of me as if I were dead.

ANNA

No, no, you weren't dead, you were so lively, so animated, you used to laugh –

DEELEY

Of course you did. I made you smile myself, didn't I? walking along the street, holding hands. You smiled fit to bust.

ANNA

Yes, she could be so . . . animated.

DEELEY

Animated is no word for it. When she smiled . . . how can I describe it?

ANNA

Her eyes lit up.

DEELEY

I couldn't have put it better myself.

DEELEY *stands, goes to cigarette box, picks it up, smiles at* KATE. KATE *looks at him, watches him light a cigarette, takes the box from him, crosses to* ANNA, *offers her a cigarette.* ANNA *takes one.*

ANNA

You weren't dead. Ever. In any way.

KATE

I said you talk about me as if I *am* dead. Now.

ANNA

How can you say that? How can you say that, when I'm looking at you now, seeing you so shyly poised over me, looking down at me –

DEELEY

Stop that!

Pause.

KATE *sits*.

DEELEY *pours a drink*.

Myself I was a student then, juggling with my future, wondering should I bejasus saddle myself with a slip of a girl not long out of her swaddling clothes whose only claim to virtue was silence but who lacked any sense of fixedness, any sense of decisiveness, but was compliant only to the shifting winds, with which she went, but not *the* winds, and certainly not my winds, such as they are, but I suppose winds that only she understood, and that of course with no understanding whatsoever, at least as I understand the word, at least that's the way I figured it. A classic female figure, I said to myself, or is it a classic female posture, one way or the other long outworn.

Pause.

That's the position as I saw it then. I mean, that is my categorical pronouncement on the position as I saw it then. Twenty years ago.

Silence.

ANNA

When I heard that Katey was married my heart leapt with joy.

DEELEY

How did the news reach you?

ANNA

From a friend.

Pause.

Yes, it leapt with joy. Because you see I knew she
never did things loosely or carelessly, recklessly. Some
people throw a stone into a river to see if the water's
too cold for jumping, others, a few others, will always
wait for the ripples before they will jump.

DEELEY

Some people do *what*? (*to* KATE) What did she say?

ANNA

And I knew that Katey would always wait not just for
the first emergence of ripple but for the ripples to
pervade and pervade the surface, for of course as you
know ripples on the surface indicate a shimmering in
depth down through every particle of water down to
the river bed, but even when she felt that happen,
when she was assured it was happening, she still might
not jump. But in this case she did jump and I knew
therefore she had fallen in love truly and was glad.
And I deduced it must also have happened to you.

DEELEY

You mean the ripples?

ANNA

If you like.

DEELEY

Do men ripple too?

ANNA

Some, I would say.

DEELEY

I see.

Pause.

ANNA

And later when I found out the kind of man you were I was doubly delighted because I knew Katey had always been interested in the arts.

KATE

I was interested once in the arts, but I can't remember now which ones they were.

ANNA

Don't tell me you've forgotten our days at the Tate? and how we explored London and all the old churches and all the old buildings, I mean those that were left from the bombing, in the City and south of the river in Lambeth and Greenwich? Oh my goodness. Oh yes. And the Sunday papers! I could never get her away from the review pages. She ravished them, and then insisted we visit that gallery, or this theatre, or that chamber concert, but of course there was so much, so much to see and to hear, in lovely London then, that sometimes we missed things, or had no more money, and so missed some things. For example, I remember one Sunday she said to me, looking up from the paper, come quick, quick, come with me quickly, and we seized our handbags and went, on a bus, to some totally obscure, totally unfamiliar district and, almost alone, saw a wonderful film called *Odd Man Out*.

Silence.

DEELEY
Yes, I do quite a bit of travelling in my job.

ANNA
Do you enjoy it?

DEELEY
Enormously. Enormously.

ANNA
Do you go far?

DEELEY
I travel the globe in my job.

ANNA
And poor Katey when you're away? What does she
do?

ANNA *looks at* KATE.

KATE
Oh, I continue.

ANNA
Is he away for long periods?

KATE
I think, sometimes. Are you?

ANNA
You leave your wife for such long periods? How can
you?

DEELEY
I have to do a lot of travelling in my job.

ANNA
(*to* KATE)

I think I must come and keep you company when he's away.

DEELEY

Won't your husband miss you?

ANNA

Of course. But he would understand.

DEELEY

Does he understand now?

ANNA

Of course.

DEELEY

We had a vegetarian dish prepared for him.

ANNA

He's not a vegetarian. In fact he's something of a gourmet We live in a rather fine villa and have done so for many years. It's very high up, on the cliffs.

DEELEY

You eat well up there, eh?

ANNA

I would say so, yes.

DEELEY

Yes, I know Sicily slightly. Just slightly. Taormina. Do you live in Taormina?

ANNA

Just outside.

Just outside, yes. Very high up. Yes, I've probably caught a glimpse of your villa.

Pause.

My work took me to Sicily. My work concerns itself with life all over, you see, in every part of the globe. With people all over the globe. I use the word globe because the word world possesses emotional political sociological and psychological pretensions and resonances which I prefer as a matter of choice to do without, or shall I say to steer clear of, or if you like to reject. How's the yacht?

ANNA

Oh, very well.

DEELEY

Captain steer a straight course?

ANNA

As straight as we wish, when we wish it

DEELEY

Don't you find England damp, returning?

ANNA

Rather beguilingly so.

DEELEY

Rather beguilingly so? (*to himself*) What the hell does she mean by that?

Pause.

Well, any time your husband finds himself in this direction my little wife will be only too glad to put the old pot on the old gas stove and dish him up something luscious if not voluptuous. No trouble.

Pause.

I suppose his business interests kept him from making the trip. What's his name? Gian Carlo or Per Paulo?

KATE
(*to* ANNA)
Do you have marble floors?

ANNA
Yes.

KATE
Do you walk in bare feet on them?

ANNA
Yes. But I wear sandals on the terrace, because it can be rather severe on the soles.

KATE
The sun, you mean? The heat.

ANNA
Yes.

DEELEY
I had a great crew in Sicily. A marvellous cameraman. Irving Shultz. Best in the business. We took a pretty austere look at the women in black. The little old women in black. I wrote the film and directed it. My name is Orson Welles.

KATE
(*to* ANNA)

Do you drink orange juice on your terrace in the morning, and bullshots at sunset, and look down at the sea?

ANNA

Sometimes, yes.

DEELEY

As a matter of fact I am at the top of my profession, as a matter of fact, and I have indeed been associated with substantial numbers of articulate and sensitive people, mainly prostitutes of all kinds.

KATE
(*to* ANNA)

And do you like the Sicilian people?

DEELEY

I've been there. There's nothing more to see, there's nothing more to investigate, nothing. There's nothing more in Sicily to investigate.

KATE
(*to* ANNA)

Do you like the Sicilian people?

ANNA *stares at her.*

Silence.

ANNA
(*quietly*)

Don't let's go out tonight, don't let's go anywhere tonight, let's stay in. I'll cook something, you can wash your hair, you can relax, we'll put on some records.

KATE

Oh, I don't know. We could go out.

ANNA

Why do you want to go out?

KATE

We could walk across the park

ANNA

The park is dirty at night, all sorts of horrible people, men hiding behind trees and women with terrible voices, they scream at you as you go past, and people come out suddenly from behind trees and bushes and there are shadows everywhere and there are policemen, and you'll have a horrible walk, and you'll see all the traffic and the noise of the traffic and you'll see all the hotels, and you know you hate looking through all those swing doors, you hate it, to see all that, all those people in the lights in the lobbies all talking and moving . . . and all the chandeliers . . .

Pause.

You'll only want to come home if you go out. You'll want to run home . . . and into your room. . . .

Pause.

KATE

What shall we do then?

ANNA

Stay in. Shall I read to you? Would you like that?

KATE

I don't know.

Pause.

ANNA

Are you hungry?

KATE

No.

DEELEY

Hungry? After that casserole?

Pause.

KATE

What shall I wear tomorrow? I can't make up my mind.

ANNA

Wear your green.

KATE

I haven't got the right top.

ANNA

You have. You have your turquoise blouse.

KATE

Do they go?

ANNA

Yes, they do go. Of course they go.

KATE

I'll try it.

Pause.

ANNA

Would you like me to ask someone over?

KATE

Who?

ANNA

Charley . . . or Jake?

KATE

I don't like Jake.

ANNA

Well, Charley . . . or . . .

KATE

Who?

ANNA

McCabe.

Pause.

KATE

I'll think about it in the bath.

ANNA

Shall I run your bath for you?

KATE
(*standing*)

No. I'll run it myself tonight.

KATE *slowly walks to the bedroom door, goes out, closes it.*

DEELEY *stands looking at* ANNA.
ANNA *turns her head towards him.*

They look at each other.

Fade.

Act Two

The bedroom.
A long window up centre. Door to bathroom up left.
Door to sitting room up right.

Two divans. An armchair.

The divans and armchair are disposed in precisely the
same relation to each other as the furniture in the first
act, but in reversed positions.

Lights dim. ANNA *discerned sitting on divan. Faint*
glow from glass panel in bathroom door.

Silence.

Lights up. The other door opens. DEELEY *comes in*
with tray.

DEELEY *comes into the room, places the tray on a table.*

DEELEY
Here we are. Good and hot. Good and strong and
hot. You prefer it white with sugar, I believe?

ANNA
Please.

DEELEY
(*pouring*)
Good and strong and hot with white and sugar.

He hands her the cup.

Like the room?

Yes.

We sleep here. These are beds. The great thing about
these beds is that they are susceptible to any amount
of permutation. They can be separated as they are
now. Or placed at right angles, or one can bisect the
other, or you can sleep feet to feet, or head to head, or
side by side. It's the castors that make all this possible.

He sits with coffee.

Yes, I remember you quite clearly from The Wayfarers.

The what?

The Wayfarers Tavern, just off the Brompton Road.

When was that?

Years ago.

I don't think so.

Oh yes, it was you, no question. I never forget a face.
You sat in the corner, quite often, sometimes alone,
sometimes with others. And here you are, sitting in my

house in the country. The same woman. Incredible.
Fellow called Luke used to go in there. You knew him.

ANNA

Luke?

DEELEY

Big chap. Ginger hair. Ginger beard.

ANNA

I don't honestly think so.

DEELEY

Yes, a whole crowd of them, poets, stunt men, jockeys,
stand-up comedians, that kind of setup. You used to
wear a scarf, that's right, a black scarf, and a black
sweater., and a skirt.

ANNA

Me?

DEELEY

And black stockings. Don't tell me you've forgotten
The Wayfarers Tavern? You might have forgotten the
name but you must remember the pub. You were the
darling of the saloon bar.

ANNA

I wasn't rich, you know. I didn't have money for
alcohol.

DEELEY

You had escorts. You didn't have to pay. You were
looked after. I bought you a few drinks myself.

ANNA

You?

DEELEY

Sure.

ANNA

Never.

DEELEY

It's the truth. I remember clearly.

Pause.

ANNA

You?

DEELEY

I've bought you drinks.

Pause.

Twenty years ago . . . or so.

ANNA

You're saying we've met before?

DEELEY

Of course we've met before.

Pause.

We've talked before. In that pub, for example. In the
corner. Luke didn't like it much but we ignored him.
Later we all went to a party. Someone's flat, somewhere
in Westbourne Grove. You sat on a very low sofa,
I sat opposite and looked up your skirt. Your black
stockings were very black because your thighs were so
white. That's something that's all over now, of course,
isn't it, nothing like the same palpable profit in it
now, it's all over. But it was worthwhile then. It was

worthwhile that night. I simply sat sipping my light
ale and gazed . . . gazed up your skirt. You didn't
object, you found my gaze perfectly acceptable.

ANNA
I was aware of your gaze, was I?

DEELEY
There was a great argument going on, about China
or something, or death, or China *and* death, I can't
remember which, but nobody but I had a thigh-kissing
view, nobody but you had the thighs which kissed.
And here you are. Same woman. Same thighs.

Pause.

Yes. Then a friend of yours came in, a girl, a girl
friend. She sat on the sofa with you, you both chatted
and chuckled, sitting together, and I settled lower to
gaze at you both, at both your thighs, squealing and
hissing, you aware, she unaware, but then a great
multitude of men surrounded me, and demanded my
opinion about death, or about China, or whatever it
was, and they would not let me be but bent down
over me, so that what with their stinking breath and
their broken teeth and the hair in their noses and
China and death and their arses on the arms of my
chair I was forced to get up and plunge my way through
them, followed by them with ferocity, as if I were the
cause of their argument, looking back through smoke,
rushing to the table with the linoleum cover to look
for one more full bottle of light ale, looking back
through smoke, glimpsing two girls on the sofa, one
of them you, heads close, whispering, no longer able to

45

see anything, no longer able to see stocking or thigh, and then you were gone. I wandered over to the sofa. There was no one on it. I gazed at the indentations of four buttocks. Two of which were yours.

Pause.

ANNA

I've rarely heard a sadder story.

DEELEY

I agree.

ANNA

I'm terribly sorry.

DEELEY

That's all right.

Pause.

I never saw you again. You disappeared from the area. Perhaps you moved out.

ANNA

No. I didn't.

DEELEY

I never saw you in The Wayfarers Tavern again. Where were you?

ANNA

Oh, at concerts, I should think, or the ballet.

Silence.

Katey's taking a long time over her bath.

DEELEY

Well, you know what she's like when she gets in the bath.

ANNA

Yes.

DEELEY

Enjoys it. Takes a long time over it.

ANNA

She does, yes.

DEELEY

A hell of a long time. Luxuriates in it. Gives herself a great soaping all over.

Pause.

Really soaps herself all over, and then washes the soap off, sud by sud. Meticulously. She's both thorough and, I must say it, sensuous. Gives herself a comprehensive going over, and apart from everything else she does emerge as clean as a new pin. Don't you think?

ANNA

Very clean.

DEELEY

Truly so. Not a speck. Not a tide mark. Shiny as a balloon.

ANNA

Yes, a kind of floating.

DEELEY

What?

ANNA

She floats from the bath. Like a dream. Unaware of anyone standing, with her towel, waiting for her, waiting to wrap it round her. Quite absorbed.

Pause.

Until the towel is placed on her shoulders.

Pause.

DEELEY

Of course she's so totally incompetent at drying herself properly, did you find that? She gives herself a really good *scrub*, but can she with the same efficiency give herself an equally good *rub*? I have found, in my experience of her, that this is not in fact the case. You'll always find a few odd unexpected unwanted cheeky globules dripping about.

ANNA

Why don't you dry her yourself?

DEELEY

Would you recommend that?

ANNA

You'd do it properly.

DEELEY

In her bath towel?

ANNA

How out?

DEELEY

How out?

ANNA

How could you dry her out? Out of her bath towel?

DEELEY

I don't know.

ANNA

Well, dry her yourself, in her bath towel.

Pause.

DEELEY

Why don't *you* dry her in her bath towel?

ANNA

Me?

DEELEY

You'd do it properly.

ANNA

No, no.

DEELEY

Surely? I mean, you're a woman, you know how and where and in what density moisture collects on women's bodies.

ANNA

No two women are the same.

DEELEY

Well, that's true enough.

Pause.

I've got a brilliant idea. Why don't we do it with powder?

49

ANNA

Is that a brilliant idea?

DEELEY

Isn't it?

ANNA

It's quite common to powder yourself after a bath.

DEELEY

It's quite common to powder yourself after a bath but it's quite uncommon to be powdered. Or is it? It's not common where I come from, I can tell you. My mother would have a fit.

Pause.

Listen. I'll tell you what. I'll do it. I'll do the whole lot The towel and the powder. After all, I am her husband. But you can supervise the whole thing. And give me some hot tips while you're at it. That'll kill two birds with one stone.

Pause.

(*to himself*) Christ.

He looks at her slowly.

You must be about forty, I should think, by now.

Pause.

If I walked into The Wayfarers Tavern now, and saw you sitting in the corner, I wouldn't recognise you.

The bathroom door opens. KATE *comes into the bedroom. She wears a bathrobe.*

She smiles at DEELEY *and* ANNA.

KATE
(*with pleasure*)
Aaahh.

She walks to the window and looks out into the night.
DEELEY *and* ANNA *watch her.*

DEELEY *begins to sing softly.*

DEELEY
(*singing*)
The way you wear your hat . . .

ANNA
(*singing, softly*)
The way you sip your tea . . .

DEELEY
(*singing*)
The memory of all that . . .

ANNA
(*singing*)
No, no, they can't take that away from me . . .

KATE *turns from the window to look at them.*

ANNA
(*singing*)
The way your smile just beams . . .

DEELEY
(*singing*)
The way you sing off key . . .

ANNA
(*singing*)
The way you haunt my dreams . . .

DEELEY
(*singing*)
No, no, they can't take that away from me . . .

KATE *walks down towards them and stands, smiling.*
ANNA *and* DEELEY *sing again, faster on cue, and more*
perfunctorily.

ANNA
(*singing*)
The way you hold your knife –

DEELEY
(*singing*)
The way we danced till three –

ANNA
(*singing*)
The way you've changed my life –

DEELEY
(*singing*)
No, no, they can't take that away from me.

KATE *sits on a divan.*

ANNA
(*to* DEELEY)
Doesn't she look beautiful?

DEELEY
Doesn't she?

KATE
Thank you. I feel fresh The water's very soft here.
Much softer than London. I always find the water
very hard in London. That's one reason I like living in

the country. Everything's softer. The water, the light, the shapes, the sounds. There aren't such edges here. And living close to the sea too. You can't say where it begins or ends. That appeals to me. I don't care for harsh lines. I deplore that kind of urgency. I'd like to go to the East, or somewhere like that, somewhere very hot, where you can lie under a mosquito net and breathe quite slowly. You know . . . somewhere where you can look through the flap of a tent and see sand, that kind of thing. The only nice thing about a big city is that when it rains it blurs everything and it blurs the lights from the cars, doesn't it, and blurs your eyes, and you have rain on your lashes. That's the only nice thing about a big city.

ANNA

That's not the only nice thing. You can have a nice room and a nice gas fire and a warm dressing gown and a nice hot drink, all waiting for you for when you come in.

Pause.

KATE

Is it raining?

ANNA

No.

KATE

Well, I've decided I will stay in tonight anyway.

ANNA

Oh good. I am glad. Now you can have a good strong cup of coffee after your bath.

ANNA *stands, goes to coffee, pours.*

I could do the hem on your black dress. I could finish it and you could try it on.

KATE

Mmmnn.

ANNA *hands her her coffee.*

ANNA

Or I could read to you.

DEELEY

Have you dried yourself properly, Kate?

KATE

I think so.

DEELEY

Are you sure? All over?

KATE

I think so. I feel quite dry.

DEELEY

Are you quite sure? I don't want you sitting here damply all over the place.

KATE *smiles.*

See that smile? That's the same smile she smiled when I was walking down the street with her, after *Odd Man Out*, well, quite some time after.

What did you think of it?

ANNA

It is a very beautiful smile.

DEELEY

Do it again.

KATE

I'm still smiling.

DEELEY

You're not. Not like you were a moment ago, not like
you did them

(*to* ANNA) You know the smile I'm talking about?

KATE

This coffee's cold.

Pause.

ANNA

Oh, I'm sorry. I'll make some fresh.

KATE

No, I don't want any, thank you.

Pause.

Is Charley coming?

ANNA

I can ring him if you like.

KATE

What about McCabe?

ANNA

Do you really want to see anyone?

KATE

I don't think I like McCabe.

ANNA

Nor do I.

KATE

He's strange. He says some very strange things to me.

ANNA

What things?

KATE

Oh, all sorts of funny things.

ANNA

I've never liked him.

KATE

Duncan's nice though, isn't he?

ANNA

Oh yes.

KATE

I like his poetry so much.

Pause.

But you know who I like best?

ANNA

Who?

KATE

Christy.

ANNA

He's lovely.

KATE

He's so gentle, isn't he? And his humour, Hasn't he
got a lovely sense of humour? And I think he's . . . so
sensitive. Why don't you ask him round?

DEELEY

He can't make it He's out of town.

KATE

Oh, what a pity.

Silence.

DEELEY
(*to* ANNA)
Am you intending to visit anyone else while you're in
England? Relations? Cousins? Brothers?

ANNA

No I know no one. Except Kate.

Pause.

DEELEY

Do you find her changed?

ANNA

Oh, just a little, not very much. (*to* KATE) You're still
shy, aren't you?

KATE *stares at her.*

(*to* DEELEY) But when I knew her first she was so shy,
as shy as a fawn, she really was. When people leaned
to speak to her she would fold away from them, so
that though she was still standing within their reach
she was no longer accessible to them. She folded

herself from them, they were no longer able to speak or go through with their touch. I put it down to her upbringing, a parson's daughter, and indeed there was a good deal of Brontë about her.

DEELEY

Was she a parson's daughter?

ANNA

But if I thought Brontë I did not think she was Brontë in passion but only in secrecy, in being so stubbornly private.

Slight pause.

I remember her first blush.

DEELEY

What? What was it? I mean why was it?

ANNA

I had borrowed some of her underwear, to go to a party. Later that night I confessed. It was naughty of me. She stared at me, nonplussed, perhaps, is the word. But I told her that in fact I had been punished for my sin, for a man at the party had spent the whole evening looking up my skirt.

Pause.

DEELEY

She blushed at that?

ANNA

Deeply.

DEELEY

Looking up *your* skirt in *her* underwear. Mmnn.

ANNA

But from that night she insisted, from time to time, that
I borrow her underwear – she had more of it than I,
and a far greater range – and each time she proposed
this she would blush, but propose it she did, nevertheless. And when there was anything to tell her, when
I got back, anything of interest to tell her, I told her.

DEELEY

Did she blush then?

ANNA

I could never see then. I would come in late and find
her reading under the lamp, and begin to tell her, but
she would say no, turn off the light, and I would tell
her in the dark. She preferred to be told in the dark.
But of course it was never completely dark, what with
the light from the gas fire or the light through the
curtains, and what she didn't know was that, knowing
her preference, I would choose a position in the room
from which I could see her face, although she could
not see mine. She could hear my voice only. And so
she listened and I watched her listening.

DEELEY

Sounds a perfect marriage.

ANNA

We were great friends.

Pause.

DEELEY

You say she was Brontë in secrecy but not in passion.
What was she in passion?

ANNA

I feel that is your province.

DEELEY

You feel it's my province? Well, you're damn right. It
is my province. I'm glad someone's showing a bit of
taste at last. Of course it's my bloody province. I'm
her husband.

Pause.

I mean I'd like to ask a question. Am I alone in
beginning to find all this distasteful?

ANNA

But what can you possibly find distasteful? I've flown
from Rome to see my oldest friend, after twenty years,
and to meet her husband. What is it that worries you?

DEELEY

What worries me is the thought of your husband
rumbling about alone in his enormous villa living
hand to mouth on a few hardboiled eggs and unable
to speak a damn word of English.

ANNA

I interpret, when necessary.

DEELEY

Yes, but you're here, with us. He's there, alone, lurching
up and down the terrace, waiting for a speedboat,
waiting for a speedboat to spill out beautiful people,
at least. Beautiful Mediterranean people. Waiting for
all *that*, a kind of elegance we know nothing about,
a slim-bellied Côte d'Azure thing we know absolutely
nothing about, a lobster and lobster sauce ideology

we know fuck-all about, the longest legs in the world,
the most phenomenally soft voices. I can hear them
now. I mean let's put it on the table, I have my eye
on a number of pulses, pulses all round the globe,
deprivations and insults, why should I waste valuable
space listening to two –

KATE
(*swiftly*)

If you don't like it go.

Pause.

DEELEY

Go? Where can I go?

KATE

To China. Or Sicily.

DEELEY

I haven't got a speedboat. I haven't got a white dinner
jacket.

KATE

China then.

DEELEY

You know what they'd do to me in China if they
found me in a white dinner jacket. They'd bloody well
kill me. You know what they're like over there.

Slight pause.

ANNA

You are welcome to come to Sicily at any time, both
of you, and be my guests.

Silence.

KATE *and* DEELEY *stare at her.*

> ANNA
> (*to* DEELEY, *quietly*)

I would like you to understand that I came here not to disrupt but to celebrate.

Pause.

To celebrate a very old and treasured friendship, something that was forged between us long before you knew of our existence.

Pause.

I found her. She grew to know wonderful people, through my introduction. I took her to cafés, almost private ones, where artists and writers and sometimes actors collected, and others with dancers, and we sat hardly breathing with our coffee, listening to the life around us. All I wanted for her was her happiness. That is all I want for her still.

Pause.

> DEELEY
> (*to* KATE)

We've met before, you know. Anna and I.

KATE *looks at him.*

Yes, we met in The Wayfarers Tavern. In the corner. She took a fancy to me. Of course I was slim-hipped in those days. Pretty nifty. A bit squinky, quite honestly. Curly hair. The lot. We had a scene together. She freaked out. She didn't have any bread, so I bought her a drink. She looked at me with big eyes, shy, all that bit. She was pretending to be you at the time. Did it pretty well. Wearing your underwear she was too, at the time. Amiably allowed me a gander. True-blue generosity. Admirable in a woman. We went to a party. Given by philosophers. Not a bad bunch. Edgware Road gang. Nice lot. Haven't seen any of them for years. Old friends. Always thinking. Spoke their thoughts. Those are the people I miss. They're all dead, anyway I've never seen them again. The Maida Vale group. Big Eric and little Tony. They lived somewhere near Paddington Library. On the way to the party I took her into a café, bought her a cup of coffee, beards with faces. She thought she was you, said little, so little. Maybe she was you. Maybe it was you, having coffee with me, saying little, so little.

Pause.

KATE

What do you think attracted her to you?

DEELEY

I don't know. What?

KATE

She found your face very sensitive, vulnerable.

DEELEY

Did she?

KATE

She wanted to comfort it, in the way only a woman can.

DEELEY

Did she?

KATE

Oh yes.

DEELEY

She wanted to comfort my face, in the way only a woman can?

KATE

She was prepared to extend herself to you.

DEELEY

I beg your pardon?

KATE

She fell in love with you.

DEELEY

With me?

KATE

You were so unlike the others. We knew men who were brutish, crass.

DEELEY

There really are such men, then? Crass men?

KATE

Quite crass.

DEELEY

But I was crass, wasn't I, looking up her skirt?

KATE

That's not crass.

DEELEY
If it was her skirt. If it was her.

ANNA
(*coldly*)
Oh, it was my skirt. It was me. I remember your look
. . . very well. I remember you well.

KATE
(*to* ANNA)
But I remember you. I remember you dead.

Pause.

I remember you lying dead. You didn't know I was
watching you. I leaned over you. Your face was dirty.
You lay dead, your face scrawled with dirt, all kinds
of earnest inscriptions, but unblotted, so that they had
run, all over your face, down to your throat. Your
sheets were immaculate. I was glad. I would have been
unhappy if your corpse had lain in an unwholesome
sheet. It would have been graceless. I mean as far as
I was concerned. As far as my room was concerned.
After all, you were dead in my room. When you woke
my eyes were above you, staring down at you. You
tried to do my little trick, one of my tricks you had
borrowed, my little slow smile, my little slow shy
smile, my bend of the head, my half-closing of the
eyes, that we knew so well, but it didn't work, the
grin only split the dirt at the sides of your mouth and
stuck. You stuck in your grin. I looked for tears but
could see none. Your pupils weren't in your eyes. Your
bones were breaking through your face. But all was
serene. There was no suffering. It had all happened

elsewhere. Last rites I did not feel necessary. Or any celebration. I felt the time and season appropriate and that by dying alone and dirty you had acted with, proper decorum. It was time for my bath. I had quite a lengthy bath, got out, walked about the room, glistening, drew up a chair, sat naked beside you and watched you.

Pause.

When I brought him into the room your body of course had gone. What a relief it was to have a different body in my room, a male body behaving quite differently, doing all those things they do and which they think are good, like sitting with one leg over the arm of an armchair. We had a choice of two beds. Your bed or my bed. To lie in, or on. To grind noses together, in or on. He liked your bed, and thought he was different in it because he was a man. But one night I said let me do something, a little thing, a little trick. He lay there in your bed. He looked up at me with great expectation. He was gratified. He thought I had profited from his teaching. He thought I was going to be sexually forthcoming, that I was about to take a long-promised initiative. I dug about in the window box, where you had planted our pretty pansies, scooped, filled the bowl, and plastered his face with dirt. He was bemused, aghast, resisted, resisted with force. He would not let me dirty his face, or smudge it, he wouldn't let me. He suggested a wedding instead and a change of environment

Slight pause.

Neither mattered.

Pause.

He asked me once, at about that time, who had slept in that bed before him. I told him no one. No one at all.

Long silence.

ANNA *stands, walks towards the door, stops, her back to them.*

Silence.

DEELEY *starts to sob, very quietly.*

ANNA *stands still.*

ANNA *turns, switches off the lamps, sits on her divan, and lies down.*

The sobbing stops.

Silence.

DEELEY *stands. He walks a few paces, looks at both divans.*

He goes to ANNA's *divan, looks down at her. She is still.*

Silence.

DEELEY *moves towards the door, stops, his back to them.*

Silence.

DEELEY *turns. He goes towards* KATE*'s divan. He sits on her divan, lies across her lap.*

Long silence.

DEELEY *very slowly sits up.*
He gets off the divan.
He walks slowly to the armchair.
He sits, slumped.

Silence.

Lights up full sharply. Very bright.

Deeley in armchair.
Anna lying on divan.
Kate sitting on divan.